S. HRG. 114–64

GLOBAL CHALLENGES AND U.S. NATIONAL SECURITY STRATEGY

HEARING

BEFORE THE

COMMITTEE ON ARMED SERVICES
UNITED STATES SENATE

ONE HUNDRED FOURTEENTH CONGRESS

FIRST SESSION

FEBRUARY 10, 2015

Printed for the use of the Committee on Armed Services

Available via the World Wide Web: http://www.fdsys.gov/

U.S. GOVERNMENT PUBLISHING OFFICE

96–248 PDF   WASHINGTON : 2015

For sale by the Superintendent of Documents, U.S. Government Publishing Office
Internet: bookstore.gpo.gov   Phone: toll free (866) 512–1800; DC area (202) 512–1800
Fax: (202) 512–2104   Mail: Stop IDCC, Washington, DC 20402–0001

COMMITTEE ON ARMED SERVICES

JOHN McCAIN, Arizona, *Chairman*

JAMES M. INHOFE, Oklahoma	JACK REED, Rhode Island
JEFF SESSIONS, Alabama	BILL NELSON, Florida
ROGER F. WICKER, Mississippi	CLAIRE McCASKILL, Missouri
KELLY AYOTTE, New Hampshire	JOE MANCHIN III, West Virginia
DEB FISCHER, Nebraska	JEANNE SHAHEEN, New Hampshire
TOM COTTON, Arkansas	KIRSTEN E. GILLIBRAND, New York
MIKE ROUNDS, South Dakota	RICHARD BLUMENTHAL, Connecticut
JONI ERNST, Iowa	JOE DONNELLY, Indiana
THOM TILLIS, North Carolina	MAZIE K. HIRONO, Hawaii
DAN SULLIVAN, Alaska	TIM KAINE, Virginia
MIKE LEE, Utah	ANGUS S. KING, JR., Maine
LINDSEY GRAHAM, South Carolina	MARTIN HEINRICH, New Mexico
TED CRUZ, Texas	

CHRISTIAN D. BROSE, *Staff Director*
ELIZABETH L. KING, *Minority Staff Director*

(II)

CONTENTS

FEBRUARY 10, 2015

(III)

GLOBAL CHALLENGES AND U.S. NATIONAL SECURITY STRATEGY

TUESDAY, FEBRUARY 10, 2015

U.S. SENATE,
COMMITTEE ON ARMED SERVICES,
Washington, DC.

The committee met, pursuant to notice, at 9:32 a.m. in room SH–216, Hart Senate Office Building, Senator John McCain (chairman) presiding.

Committee members present: Senators McCain, Inhofe, Sessions, Wicker, Ayotte, Cotton, Rounds, Ernst, Tillis, Sullivan, Reed, Nelson, Manchin, Shaheen, Gillibrand, Blumenthal, Donnelly, Hirono, Kaine, King, and Heinrich.

OPENING STATEMENT OF SENATOR JOHN McCAIN, CHAIRMAN

Chairman McCAIN. Good morning.

Since a quorum is now present, I would ask the committee to consider the nomination of Dr. Ashton B. Carter to be Secretary of Defense, and if a roll call is requested, we would be glad to have a roll call. If not, is there a motion to—is there anyone who would like a roll call vote?

Senator MANCHIN. Yes.

Chairman McCAIN. You want a roll call vote?

Senator MANCHIN. I want a roll call vote.

Chairman McCAIN. Yes, I don't know if we need it.

Senator REED. We don't need it.

Senator WICKER. Mr. Chairman, I would like to be recorded as voting aye.

Chairman McCAIN. The clerk will call the roll.

The CLERK. Mr. Inhofe?

Senator INHOFE. Aye.

The CLERK. Mr. Sessions?

Senator SESSIONS. Aye.

The CLERK. Mr. Wicker?

Senator WICKER. Aye.

The CLERK. Ms. Ayotte?

Senator AYOTTE. Aye.

The CLERK. Mrs. Fischer?

Chairman McCAIN. Aye, by proxy.

The CLERK. Mr. Cotton?

Senator COTTON. Aye.

The CLERK. Mr. Rounds?

Senator ROUNDS. Aye.

The CLERK. Mrs. Ernst?

Senator ERNST. Aye.

The CLERK. Mr. Tillis?

Senator TILLIS. Aye.

The CLERK. Mr. Sullivan?

Chairman MCCAIN. No instructions.

The CLERK. Mr. Lee?

Chairman MCCAIN. Aye, by proxy.

The CLERK. Mr. Graham?

Chairman MCCAIN. Aye, by proxy.

The CLERK. Mr. Cruz?

Chairman MCCAIN. Aye, by proxy.

The CLERK. Mr. Reed?

Senator REED. Aye.

The CLERK. Mr. Nelson?

Senator REED. Aye, by proxy.

The CLERK. Mrs. McCaskill?

Senator REED. Aye, by proxy.

The CLERK. Mr. Manchin?

Senator MANCHIN. Aye.

The CLERK. Mrs. Shaheen?

Senator SHAHEEN. Aye.

The CLERK. Mrs. Gillibrand?

Senator GILLIBRAND. Aye.

The CLERK. Mr. Blumenthal?

Senator BLUMENTHAL. Aye.

The CLERK. Mr. Donnelly?

Senator DONNELLY. Aye.

The CLERK. Ms. Hirono?

Senator REED. Aye, by proxy.

The CLERK. Mr. Kaine?

Senator REED. Aye, by proxy.

The CLERK. Mr. King?

Senator KING. Aye.

The CLERK. Mr. Heinrich?

Senator HEINRICH. Aye.

The CLERK. Mr. Chairman?

Chairman MCCAIN. Aye.

The CLERK. 25 ayes, 1 no instruction.

Chairman MCCAIN. Then the motion will be reported favorably of Dr. Carter's nomination to the Senate—to the floor of the Senate, and hopefully, we can get a vote perhaps even as early as tomorrow.

Senator REED. Do you want to keep it open for Senator Sullivan?

Chairman MCCAIN. For who?

Senator REED. Senator Sullivan.

Chairman MCCAIN. No.

We will leave it open for Senator Sullivan to make his wishes known for a while.

The Armed Services Committee meets today to receive testimony on our Nation's defense budget and priorities from the bipartisan National Defense Panel (NDP). This group of former military leaders, Members of Congress, and Pentagon officials who served under Republican and Democratic Presidents released their unanimous recommendations in a report on our Nation's defense strategy last year.

We have with us today two distinguished members of the NDP, Eric Edelman and Michéle Flournoy. Each served as Under Secretary of Defense for Policy and are among the most respected defense experts on both sides of the aisle. We are grateful for you to appear before us today.

I would also like to thank the panel's co-chairmen, Dr. William Perry and General John Abizaid, for their leadership, as well as the panel's members and staff for their diligent work.

The NDP's bipartisan and consensus report is a compelling statement of the daunting strategic realities America faces in the 21st century. The rules-based international order that has furthered global prosperity and security is not self-sustaining. As challenges to that order multiply around the world, there is no substitute for robust American engagement to ensure its preservation. Though America has many effective tools of global influence, including diplomacy and economic engagement, the panel reminds us that all of these are critically intertwined with and dependent upon the perceived strength, presence, and commitment of U.S. Armed Forces.

Yet through a combination of self-inflicted wounds and dangerous geopolitical and technological trends, America's military strength, ''the strategic foundation undergirding our global leadership'' as the report terms it, is eroding.

$487 billion in cuts to our national defense under the Budget Control Act (BCA) of 2011 and billions more under sequestration constitute a serious strategic misstep, the report warns. These steep cuts have sharply reduced military readiness, led to dangerous investment shortfalls in present and future capabilities, and prompted our allies and adversaries alike to question our commitment and resolve.

These cuts are not the product of any strategic assessment of the threats we face at a time of global upheaval. China's rapid military modernization is tilting the balance of power in the Asia-Pacific. Russia's aggression threatens Europe's regional security. Iran and North Korea continue the pursuit and development of tactical weapons, and violent Islamist extremists are destabilizing large swaths of the Middle East and North Africa while plotting attacks against the United States and our allies.

In addition to regional threats, structural trends like the diffusion of certain advanced military technologies pose new operations challenges to America's Armed Forces. In the security environment of the future, the panel's report predicts, ''Conflicts are likely to unfold more rapidly. Battlefields will be more lethal. Operational sanctuary for U.S. forces will be scarce and often fleeting. Asymmetric conflict will be the norm.''

The panel echoed Secretary of Defense, Charles T. Hagel, who has said that in such an era, American dominance on the seas and the skies and in space can no longer be taken for granted.

The panel's report recommends the BCA's immediate repeal and a return to at least the funding baseline proposed in Secretary of Defense, Robert M. Gates' fiscal year 2012 defense budget. That budget, the panel concluded, represents the last time the Department was permitted to engage in the standard process of analyzing threats, estimating needs, and proposing a resource baseline that would permit it to carry out the national military strategy.

If we had followed the budget path laid out by Secretary Gates, which he believed was the minimum to keep the country safe, the fiscal year 2016 budget for the Department of Defense (DOD), excluding war funding, would be $611 billion. That is $77 billion more than the President's fiscal year 2016 budget request, and $112 billion more than the budget caps under the BCA.

It is also worth remembering that Secretary Gates suggested this minimum level before Russia's invasion of Ukraine posed a renewed threat to European security, before the rise of the Islamic State of Iraq and the Levant (ISIS) and the further spread of violent extremism across North Africa and the Middle East, before China's coercive behavior in the East and South China Seas had become dangerously commonplace.

It is unacceptable to continue to ask the men and women of our military to put their lives at risk around the world while we cut back on their training and equipment to settle domestic political scores. Therefore, the overriding priority of this committee and Congress must be to return to a strategy-driven budget. I look forward to the testimony of our witnesses today as to what budget would look like.

Senator Reed?

STATEMENT OF SENATOR JACK REED

Senator REED. Well, thank you very much, Mr. Chairman.

I also want to welcome our witnesses. Mr. Ambassador, Madam Secretary, thank you for your service both in and out of Government. Thank you very much.

Over the years, and especially since the initiation of hostilities in 2001, the Quadrennial Defense Review (QDR), like any strategy, has had to contend with the challenge of an unpredictable and constantly shifting nature of the world and threats that we face. As military leaders have pointed out, we have seldom predicted with great accuracy where or when the next crisis might occur.

However, DOD's requirement to conduct security and defense analysis and planning means that assumptions must be made, objective threat assessments done, and guidance provided to our military leaders that prioritize our national security interests. Each QDR, regardless of administration, has had to make strategic or resource tradeoffs.

The work of the current NDP, in its review of the 2014 QDR, provides an independent consideration of the department's assessment of the security environment, its defense strategy and priorities, and identification of the capabilities necessary to manage our strategic risk.

In essence, the panel found that the 2014 QDR and defense strategy makes a reasonable strategic assessment. For example, the panel largely echoes the QDR's strategic assessment and highlights the challenges the Nation faces, with emphasis on China, Russia in Ukraine, proliferation in North Korea and Iran, insurgency in Iraq, civil war in Syria, and instability throughout the Middle East and Africa.

The panel also acknowledges that the QDR calls for the right capabilities and capacities to address the many challenges we face today and into the future. However, the panel notes, those capabilities and capacities clearly exceed the budget resources available and, therefore, undermines the strategy. A point very accurately made by the chairman.

It is no surprise, therefore, that the panel's overarching finding and recommendation is the BCA endangers the Nation's security and calls for its repeal. The panel also argues for increasing defense funding to 2012 levels, reining in personnel costs, and more budget predictability. In addition to the risks of sequestration, I would be interested to hear the witnesses' assessment of other risks to our national security, as well as well as risks to our military and their families.

Finally, Mr. Chairman, I note that after nearly 20 years of QDRs and recurring questions about its value, last year's National Defense Authorization Act modified the requirements for this periodic defense review, now called the Defense Strategy Review. These changes include the development of a national defense strategy that addresses our security interest across the near, mid, and far terms, and focuses and streamlines the elements of a strategy Congress considers essential to a comprehensive defense review.

I would be interested to know the witnesses' views on these changes and the prospects for a more timely, relevant, and useful national defense strategy process.

Thank you, Mr. Chairman.

Chairman McCAIN. Welcome to the witnesses. Secretary Flournoy?

Ms. FLOURNOY. Sir, if I may, I am going to let Ambassador Edelman go first.

STATEMENT OF HON. ERIC S. EDELMAN, PANELIST, NATIONAL DEFENSE PANEL AND FORMER UNDER SECRETARY OF DEFENSE FOR POLICY

Ambassador EDELMAN. Mr. Chairman, Senator Reed, thank you for giving my colleague, Secretary Flournoy, and me an opportunity to come before you to talk about the work of the NDP to review the QDR. The two of us have a prepared statement that we have submitted and hope that it will be printed for the record.

Chairman McCAIN. Without objection, they are both in the record.

Ambassador EDELMAN. I will just make some general introductory comments and then turn the floor over to Michéle.

When we began our work as a panel in August 2013, one of our co-chairmen, General John Abizaid, said that as we started our deliberations that he believed the Nation was running what he called accumulating strategic risk. I think all of the members of the panel assented to that judgment at the time.

As you pointed out in your opening statement, Mr. Chairman, that was before President Putin had invaded and annexed Crimea and destabilized Eastern Ukraine, before the collapse of the Iraqi security forces and the seizure of Mosul and Anbar Province by ISIL and its approach to Baghdad. As we went through our deliberations, I think the panel became more and more convinced that the accumulating strategic risk that General Abizaid was describing at our outset was accumulating at a faster and faster pace.

As you have heard as a committee from previous witnesses at other hearings—Secretary George P. Shultz, my former boss; Secretary Henry A. Kissinger, and Secretary Madeleine K. Albright—the United States probably faces the most volatile and complex security environment that we have faced as a nation in a very long time, if ever. It struck us as a panel that, given those growing challenges, to stay on the path of the BCA caps and sequestration made no sense.

I had the experience of having been on the previous independent panel to review the 2010 QDR, and in that report looking at the budget trajectory, the cuts that were already being taken out of defense in 2010, the growing cost of keeping service men and women in the field over time, and the growing healthcare and other retirement costs that were built into the budget, we predicted that the Nation was facing a train wreck on defense. That was before the BCA passed and before the department had to cope with sequestration.

One of the things that I think we were very focused on and I want draw some attention to is the charge that Secretary Hagel gave us as a panel at the outset of our deliberations. He said that as we discussed future capabilities, because many of these challenges that we as a panel were talking about—the rise of China and its very rapid growth in military power, the long struggle I think that we face with Islamic extremism, the rise potentially of new nuclear powers like North Korea, perhaps Iran—all of these things are challenges that, as President Dwight D. Eisenhower said, were for the long haul. We have to think now about how we are going to deal with these challenges 20 years out. That, in fact, is also one of the mandates of the QDR process itself. It is supposed to be a 20-year-out look at the Nation's defense needs.

So, Secretary Hagel raised the issue with us, the concern that is the program of record the program we are going to need 20 years down the road? Are we going to be starting now to produce the weapons that 20 years from now we will be needing?

Many of us, I think, were mindful of the fact that over the last decade we have been essentially eating the seed corn that was laid down in the President James E. Carter and President Ronald W. Reagan defense build-up of the late 1970s and early 1980s. So, we need to be thinking now of what capabilities we can provide for service men and women who are going to be called upon in the future.

So, I wanted to mention the specific areas that as a panel, in keeping with Secretary Hagel's charge, that we concluded we ought to be looking at down the road for the future. I hope, Mr. Chairman and Senator Reed, that you and the members of the committee will bearing some of those things in mind as you consider the program and budget review over the next few years.

I will just tick them off. Armed intelligence surveillance and reconnaissance. Space, because of our critical dependence on it. Cyberspace. Maintenance of air superiority. Joint and coalition command and control, because of the partnerships we have and the fact we are going to be fighting with other people. Long-range strike, and electric and directed-energy weapons.

These are areas that we felt had not been given sufficient attention by the department and need a further look in the future.

Why don't I stop there, and I will be happy to turn it over to Michéle.

[The joint prepared statement of Ambassador Edelman and Ms. Flournoy follows:]

STATEMENT OF HON. MICHÉLE A. FLOURNOY, PANELIST, NATIONAL DEFENSE PANEL AND FORMER UNDER SECRETARY OF DEFENSE FOR POLICY

Ms. FLOURNOY. Mr. Chairman, Senator Reed, I would just like to say how pleased and honored I am to join Ambassador Edelman here today to discuss the findings and recommendations of the NDP with you.

This hearing really could not come at a more critical time for all the reasons you have described. The international security environment is more complex and volatile than we have seen, and I would emphasize it is only going to get more challenging in the future.

It is a time when continued U.S. leadership and engagement globally to protect our national interests, to sustain the rules-based international order on which stability and prosperity depend, to lead the international community to address the most pressing challenges that you outline, U.S. leadership could not be at more of a premium right now.

It is also a time that requires investment to ensure that we retain a strong and agile military to shape the international environment, to deter and defeat aggression when we must, to reassure allies and partners, and to ensure that this President and future Presidents have the options that they need for an increasingly dangerous world. Yet, we see a period where defense budget cuts and sequestration are undermining the department's ability to maintain a robust and ready force, to retain the best and brightest people, and to invest in the capabilities that are going to be necessary to keep our technological edge and our military superiority in a more challenging future.

So, in this context, I just want to foot stomp and emphasize four points.

First is, our number-one appeal to this committee and to Congress more broadly is to work to repeal the BCA and end sequestration. This is absolutely imperative. We cannot restore readiness and invest in our technological edge unless we do so.

Sequestration not only sets budget levels too low, it also denies the Secretary of Defense the ability to protect resources for the highest priorities. It puts DOD in a constant state of budget uncertainty that prevents more strategic planning and investment for the future.

Deficit reduction and getting our fiscal house in order are essential to U.S. national security. But sequestration is the wrong way to go about it. So the NDP does recommend restoring defense spending to fiscal year 2012 levels, as the chairman mentioned, and funding the President's budget request is at least a first step in that direction.

Second, we would urge Congress to take immediate steps to restore readiness. The Service Chiefs have testified before this committee as to growing readiness problems. Only half of the Marine Corps home station units are at acceptable readiness levels. Less than half of the combat-coded units in the Air Force are fully ready for their missions. Navy deployments have been cancelled, and only a third of the Navy's contingency force is ready to deploy within the required 30 days.

The list goes on. These readiness impacts are real, and the NDP recommended that Congress should make an immediate and special appropriation above and beyond the current budget levels and Overseas Contingency Operations to correct these readiness shortfalls.

Third, as Ambassador Edelman emphasized, the NDP calls for protecting investment in future capabilities that will be critical to maintaining U.S. freedom of action and our military superiority in the coming decades. Our technological edge has long been an advantage, but it is not a given. In a world in which technology is proliferating, much of cutting-edge technology is commercial and off the shelf. DOD has to have a smart and determined investment strategy to maintain its edge.

I would personally applaud the Department's efforts like the offset strategy, the Defense Innovation Initiative, but we have to have the investment dollars to pursue those initiatives, and Ambassador Edelman has laid out a number of the key areas that the NDP recommended should be a focus.

Lastly, I would add the NDP also argues that we need to pursue an aggressive reform agenda inside DOD. We can and should reduce the costs of doing business. We note compensation reform and applauded the work of the Military Compensation and Retirement Modernization Commission.

Many of these issues need to be addressed. Some of them need to be fundamentally reframed, and I will give you an example. Healthcare, for example, rather than debating whether we should reduce benefits and increase co-pays, we need to be debating how do we get better health outcomes for servicemembers and their families and reduce costs by applying better business practices.

The NDP emphasizes the need for further acquisition reform, for another Defense Base Realignment and Closure round to take down the 20 percent excess infrastructure that the DOD is carrying, and to right-sizing the civilian workforce—contractor, career, and so forth—so that we can have the workforce we need for the future.

Let me just conclude by saying I think this report lays out an agenda, a very clear agenda, for action that had strong bipartisan and civil-military support across the panel. Nevertheless, there are some heavy lifts involved in what we recommend. But the risks of not pursuing this course are simply unacceptable. So I would look to this committee and applaud your leadership in this area, working with your colleagues to try to convince them that the time to act on these recommendations is now.

Thank you.

Joint Prepared Statement by Michele Flournoy and Eric Edelman

Chairman McCain and Ranking Member Reed, thank you for this opportunity to appear before you and other members of this distinguished committee to discuss the final report of the 2014 Quadrennial Defense Review (QDR) National Defense Panel.

The 2014 QDR National Defense Panel, which included two appointees of the Secretary of Defense and eight appointees of Congress, and was facilitated by the U.S. Institute of Peace, had been asked to submit a written assessment of the QDR. We are here today as the designated representative of the co-chairs, former Secretary of Defense William J. Perry and General (Retired) John P Abizaid, to discuss with you the Panel's report which was released on July 31, 2014.

Mr. Chairman, our panel observed recent events across the globe—from the rise of the Islamic State, Russia's invasion of Ukraine, war between Hamas and Israel, violent confrontations and air strikes in Libya, and continued tensions on the Korean Peninsula and in the East and South China seas—and was reminded that the United States faces perhaps the most complex and volatile security environment since World War II.

This realization has led to repeated calls for U.S. leadership to sustain the rules-based international order that underpins U.S. security and prosperity. But scant attention has been paid to ensuring that we have a robust and ready military, able to deter would-be aggressors, reassure allies and ensure that any president, current or future, has the options he or she will need in an increasingly dangerous world.

The National Defense Panel concluded in its recent report that the Budget Control Act of 2011 was a "serious strategic misstep" that has dangerously tied the hands of the Pentagon leadership, forcing across-the-board "sequestration" cuts in defense spending and subjecting the Nation to accumulating strategic risk. The commission's report concluded that, without budgetary relief, the U.S. Armed Forces soon will be at high risk of not being able to accomplish the national defense strategy. The panel also believes if the United States returns to sequestration-level cuts in fiscal year 2016, we will face significant risks across the board, and may have to reassess our defense strategy.

The provisions of the Budget Control Act and sequestration have already precipitated a readiness crisis within our Armed Forces, with only a handful of Army brigades ready for crisis response, Air Force pilots unable to fly sufficient hours to keep up their skills and Navy ships unable to provide critical U.S. security presence in key regions. We also understand that the Department has reported that if sequestration returns in fiscal year 2016, the Navy would be unable to support its current force of 11 carriers. we note with grave concern the statement Dr. Ashton Carter, the nominee for secretary of defense, made at his hearing when he noted that sequestration threatens Department of Defense modernization and that in turn would threaten our Asia-Pacific rebalance strategy. Although last year's congressional budget deal has granted some temporary relief, the return to sequestration in fiscal year 2016 and beyond would result in a hollow force reminiscent of the late 1970s.

The U.S. military is an indispensable instrument underpinning the diplomatic, economic and intelligence elements of our national power: It keeps key trade routes open, maintains stability in vital regions such as the Persian Gulf and sustains alliances that serve U.S. and global interests.

That's why the National Defense Panel urged—and we reiterate today—that Congress and the President repeal the Budget Control Act immediately, end the threat of sequestration and return, at a minimum, to funding levels proposed by then-Defense Secretary Robert Gates in his fiscal year 2012 budget. That budget called for modest nominal-dollar increases in defense spending through the remainder of the decade to stabilize the defense program.

The report argues that, to meet the increasing challenges of the deteriorating international security environment, the U.S. military must be able to deter or stop aggression in multiple theaters, not just one, even when engaged in a large-scale war. This requires urgently addressing the size and shape of our Armed Forces so they can protect and advance our interests globally and provide the warfighting capabilities necessary to underwrite the credibility of the United States' leadership and national security strategy. But under sequestration, our forces would have to accept a much higher level of risk in order to implement our current strategies.

Whether confronting the threat of the Islamic State or reassuring allies in Asia, the President must have options, and the Defense Department needs the flexibility to provide the best alternatives that secure our interests. In particular, the Pentagon needs relief from the budget cuts of the past few years and from limitations on its authority to make judicious cuts where they are most needed and least harmful to our security. This would allow further savings through modest cuts to the rate of growth in already generous military compensation and benefits, further reforms in the acquisition of equipment and materiel, elimination of an estimated 20 percent excess in military infrastructure such as bases, and reductions in overhead and the burgeoning civilian and contractor defense workforce.

These savings and additional budgetary resources must go toward investment in critical capabilities, such as long-range strikes, armed unmanned aviation, intelligence surveillance and reconnaissance, undersea warfare, directed energy, cybersecurity, and others that will safeguard our continued military superiority.

The threat of sequester was never meant to be carried out. It was supposed to be a ''sword of Damocles'' ensuring that lawmakers would reach an agreement on ways to cut the Federal deficit. Those efforts failed, putting the defense budget on the chopping block and holding our Nation's security hostage at a particularly dangerous moment in world affairs. As we enter another presidential election cycle, our Nation's leaders will need to examine

the National Defense Panel report and explain to voters how they intend to address its recommendations. The stakes could not be higher.

Mr. Chairman, thank you for the opportunity to appear before you today. We welcome your questions and input regarding the 2014 Quadrennial Defense Review National Defense Panel.

Chairman McCAIN. I thank both the witnesses, and I would point out to my colleagues that both witnesses have worked for both Republican and Democrat administrations, holding positions of responsibility in both. So there certainly is a total nonpartisanship in your reports, and that, in my view, makes you even more credible because of your many years of outstanding and dedicated service.

My colleagues, I won't take very much time except to point out that one of the problems that we are trying to highlight on this committee is, as you just mentioned, Ms. Flournoy, on acquisition reform. We simply can't afford these cost overruns of billions of dollars and cancelled and delayed programs.

It harms our credibility, and it is going to be one of the highest priorities of this committee to try and address that issue, and it has been tried many times in the past. So I am not confident as to the degree of success, but we have to work on it.

I only have one additional question. Why did you use Secretary Gates' fiscal year 2012 budget levels as a baseline for your recommendations?

Ambassador EDELMAN. Mr. Chairman, as I mentioned, in the 2010 NDP, we spoke to Secretary Gates about what he thought the department needed to recapitalize after 10 years of war. He told us that he believed he needed about 1.5 to 2.5 percent real growth in the budget over the Future Years Defense Program in order to do that.

I think the 2010 Panel believed that that was a minimum and that it might actually be a higher number. But when we met as a panel and tried to wrestle with this—and we had a smaller panel this time, only 10 members and limited staff—we concluded that recurring to Secretary Gates' top line made sense because it was really the last time the department had been trying to define its needs on the basis of something approaching a strategy, as opposed to being given arbitrary numbers by either the DOD Office of Management and Budget or because of the BCA caps.

So there were differences of view, I think, among us on the panel as to what, how high the top line ought to go. But I think there was consensus that the Gates level, that sort of 1.5, 2.5 percent real growth from the fiscal year 2011 and fiscal year 2012 levels, was the minimum, and all of us could agree on that.

Chairman MCCAIN. Unless we do something such as you are recommending, the Nation's security is at risk.

Ambassador EDELMAN. I would say so, and I think—I think all the members of the panel believed that.

Ms. FLOURNOY. Yes, sir, I think we talked about the force being at substantial risk in the near term if sequestration was not lifted and higher budget levels not restored.

Chairman MCCAIN. Thank you.

Senator Reed?

Senator REED. Thank you very much, Mr. Chairman.

Thank you, Ambassador and Madam Secretary, for your thoughtful testimony today and also for the work of your colleagues on this report.

You were obviously tasked with focusing on the needs and responsibilities of DOD, but one of the realities I think we all recognize is that military forces don't operate alone, and they are a part of a spectrum of national security efforts. If there is not a sufficient State Department presence and capacity building in local communities, then our military efforts could dissipate quickly when we change or shift responsibility.

So can I assume, or I won't assume, but I will just ask, when we talk about repealing the BCA, we also have to be conscious of the State Department, Homeland Security Department, every agency of the Government that essentially protects the security of the United States and could even go further than that.

Is that fair, Mr. Ambassador?

Ambassador EDELMAN. Senator Reed, I think that is certainly fair. Although we in our panel really were more focused on the department specifically, in the 2010 Panel, we actually had a chapter about the need for a better whole-of-government effort, really very much along the lines you are discussing.

Because you are right, just solving DOD's problem is crucial and, I would say, a necessary condition for almost everything else. But it is not sufficient because we have other instruments of national power that we don't want to see withering on the vine without adequate funding.

Senator REED. Madam Secretary, your comment?

Ms. FLOURNOY. I would agree. In just about every operation we conduct, every problem we try to solve, there has to be an integrated, balanced interagency approach. When one instrument is well funded and the others are on life support, that doesn't work so well. So I think our intention was to talk about the instruments of national security more broadly.

Senator REED. Let me shift to another topic that you talked about in your report, which is increasingly critical. That is cyber operations. It just, from afar, looking at some of the recent operations of the Russians in the Crimea, et cetera, that cyber seems to be the first act of any sort of military operation today. The line between a cyber incident and a military operation is getting less and less distinct.

Your comments generally about the efforts we should undertake with respect to cyber through the DOD and others? Again, this touches the whole spectrum. Everything is cyber these days.

Ambassador EDELMAN. Senator Reed, I am at something of a disadvantage because I have trouble booting up my own computer, and I am like many people of my age, very reliant on my younger sons to get me out of trouble.

Senator REED. Or grandkids.

Ambassador EDELMAN. But the reality is we rely, our military forces rely, extensively on cyber and not only encrypted systems, but on the open Net. That is a huge problem for us whenever we are involved in an operation of any kind, and I think we are all painfully aware of the vulnerabilities that we face. We do cite cyber as one of the capabilities that needs further attention and a lot more work.

But you have put your finger on one problem that I don't think we have completely resolved as a government. My colleague may have more recent experience with this. But as I said, DOD relies on the open Internet, and yet it doesn't really have the responsibility for defending it. It has the responsibility for defending dot-mil. So, we really have to—this is one area where the whole of government has to be involved, particularly for DOD.

Senator REED. Madam Secretary?

Ms. FLOURNOY. I would just add I think it is a very important area of emphasis, and there are many dimensions to the challenge. One is building the human capital and the expertise that is needed within the Government, and access to it outside of Government. Figuring out how we are going to organize ourselves beyond DOD, across the whole of government, given that different agencies have different authorities and areas of expertise.

How we are going to work with the private sector, which now holds so much of our critical infrastructure. Frankly, the legislative framework that deals with questions of liability and otherwise that would enable the kind of public-private cooperation that is needed to be effective in this area.

Senator REED. Thank you very much. Thank you for your great work.

Thank you, Mr. Chairman.

Chairman MCCAIN. Senator Inhofe?

Senator INHOFE. Thank you, Mr. Chairman.

Ambassador, when you are my age, you will be depending on your grandchildren's advice, not just your children's.

In the 20 years that I have been on this committee, we have talked about our—and you and I have talked about this, too, about the fact that we have the oldest nuclear arsenal in the world, that most of our warheads are 30, 40 years old, and our delivery systems, if you look at the Triad, you are looking at the B–52, maybe 50 years old. Then, of course, the intercontinental ballistic missiles and the nuclear submarines.

Now we have talked about this for a long period of time, and I am looking now at the new situation, the new threat that is out there, the new threat that you have talked about, both of you, as well as our panel that we had last week that talked about this for quite some time—Kissinger, Albright, and Shultz. Now in light of the new threat, should more attention be given to this than we have in the past?

I notice when you used the word, you ticked off five of the areas that have not been given proper attention. This wasn't one of those areas. Well, do you think it should be?

Ambassador EDELMAN. Senator, as Under Secretary, I was a member of the Nuclear Weapons Council and followed the issues closely and was very, very concerned throughout my tenure about the state of our aging nuclear force. We haven't built a new nuclear weapon since 1988. We haven't tested one since 1991.

There are lots of ways that we maintain the safety and surety of the stockpile. But as time goes on, and particularly not only as the inevitable corrosion and degradation of components goes on, but also the loss of human capital, because we are not able to get the best and brightest minds in the field the way we used to be able to do, I think it is a matter of really increasing concern.

We are unfortunately, I think, living through a period where the risks of an increasingly proliferated world are growing. We already have North Korea testing, having tested nuclear weapons. Iran is moving very close to being a nuclear threshold state. Hopefully, there will be an agreement that will constrain that. But if there isn't or if Iran maintains a near-breakout capacity, there is a real prospect that we may get other states in the region who decide to develop their own nuclear capabilities.

In the meantime, you have growing nuclear stockpiles in Pakistan and India. China's—the Chinese inventory is also growing in terms of weapons, although albeit more slowly. Russia is modernizing its nuclear force.

I do worry. I think I applaud the administration for the very good work it has done and the B–61 modernization effort. But I do think there is much more that needs to be done in this area.

Senator INHOFE. Well, Ambassador, that gets into what I was going to talk about because I have been concerned about Iran for ever since our unclassified intelligence came out in 2007 talking about when they were going to have the capabilities, being 2015, which is where we are right now.

I am concerned about the maligned activities. There have been several published reports talking about Sudan—this is all coming from Iran—Sudan, Gaza, Yemen, Bahrain, Iraq, Syria, and Lebanon. I don't think we can assume that our concern should be strictly with Iran. This is my concern that I have had for a long time.

We are supposed to be, and historically have been, the nuclear umbrella. Our umbrella has holes in it. We have serious problems.

When you look at countries like Saudi Arabia and Turkey and others, if they see what our capabilities aren't, then you know, or I would assume, they are going to be involved and we are going to have another arms race coming up. Does that concern the two of you?

Ambassador EDELMAN. I think our strategic nuclear forces have been one of our huge strategic comparative advantages as a nation since 1945.

Senator INHOFE. Yes.

Ambassador EDELMAN. I think we cannot afford to let that advantage go by the wayside. Extended deterrence of our allies in Asia, in Europe, and now increasingly in the Middle East has always been a very difficult proposition. It was a difficult proposition when we had a much larger stockpile and inventory of nuclear weapons to make our willingness to use those weapons in defense of our allies. That was a very difficult proposition to convince people of.

It is still going to be a difficult proposition to convince people about. But it will be much harder to do, as you say, Senator Inhofe, if the appearance is that we are not paying sufficient attention to the stockpile and to the modernization of our forces.

Senator INHOFE. All right. Well, thank you.

My time is expired, but just as I did for the panel of Kissinger, Albright, and Shultz, I would like to have you submit, for the record, something talking about the fact that for the 20 years that we were—I was involved with this committee, before we had the policy of being able to fight two wars or two major theater conflicts, and that policy seemingly changing now, and your analysis of the new policy for the record.

Thank you, Mr. Chairman.

[The information referred to follows:]

Ambassador Edelman did not respond in time for printing. When received, answer will be retained in committee files.

Chairman MCCAIN. Senator Sullivan, do you wish to be recorded as voting aye for Ash Carter to be Secretary of Defense?

Senator SULLIVAN. Yes, Mr. Chairman.

Chairman MCCAIN. Great. Senator Gillibrand?

Senator GILLIBRAND. Thank you, Mr. Chairman. Thank you, Senator Reed.

Thank you for your testimony today. It is very instructive and something that obviously this committee is really focused on.

I want to continue the conversation about your recommendations with regard to cyber. Obviously, the 2014 QDR reports that cyber threats come from a diverse range of countries, organizations, individuals and are posing significant risks to U.S. national interests. Some threats seek to undercut DOD's near- and long-term military effectiveness by gaining unauthorized access to the DOD and industry networks and infrastructure on a routine basis.

Further, our potential adversaries are actively probing critical infrastructure, whether they are chemical plants, nuclear plants, stock exchanges, any type of important infrastructure, and our partner countries, which could inflict significant damage to the global economy as well as exacerbate instability in the security environment.

What are your specific recommendations with regard to increasing cyber capability, and specifically, how do we compete with the private sector to get the brightest minds, the best engineers, the best mathematicians to want to serve as cyber warriors to enhance our cyber defense?

Have you thought about ways to not only recruit and retain the best and brightest in these fields, but also to perhaps develop resources throughout National Guard and other sources?

Ms. FLOURNOY. As a panel, Senator, we did not go into that level of detail. We noted the importance of this area, the importance of investing in both defensive and offensive capabilities. Urged the department to move forward with modernization and improving cooperation with the private sector. So I will give you my personal views on your question. I think attracting talent is one of the biggest challenges, and there are a couple of ways to go at it.

One is to use different incentives and pay schedules for cyber experts than the normal GS kind of schedule.

A second is to develop contract relationships and surge capacity with the private sector.

A third is, as you mentioned, actually leveraging some of the strength of our Guard and Reserves. There are a lot of these folks who have this expertise out in the commercial sector who are patriots and who might want to contribute to our national defense, but they are not going to leave Silicon Valley to join full time. So finding a way to leverage them on the weekends and for their annual training and to be available to be mobilized in a national emergency, I think we need to be thinking creatively about those kinds of arrangements.

A couple of the Services have some pilot programs that you may be aware of, experimenting with exactly that construct. But the human capital dimension is probably the long pole in the tent here.

Ambassador EDELMAN. Senator Gillibrand, the only thing that I would to add to that, I am aware of some efforts in the private sector to do something which I think is in this context a terrific idea, which is to help train some of our wounded warriors to become cyber warriors. There are a lot of our wounded warriors who would love to get back into the field, but because of their injuries cannot. But this is a way for them to continue the fight with a little bit of training.

Senator GILLIBRAND. Well, would you recommend, for example, our cyber defenders or our cyber fighters to not have the same basic training? Meaning, you might be the best person behind a computer, but you are not the best guy behind a gun, and so train specifically for their requirements. But that would be the first for the military. They have not done that previously.

Ms. FLOURNOY. My understanding is that at least one of the pilots that is using a Reserve unit, one of the things they have done is exempt people from the physical training requirements, from cutting their hair, wearing uniforms. But really let them come as they are, bring their expertise to the table without having to meet the traditional requirements.

Senator GILLIBRAND. Then, in your opening remarks, Ambassador, you mentioned five various technology areas where you felt we need to develop more weapons expertise. Does your report expand on that, or do you just list them?

Ambassador EDELMAN. We don't go into great detail, Senator Gillibrand, about them. We basically highlight them as areas where we clearly think there needs to be more attention, and there hasn't been sufficient attention. Directed-energy weapons for one. But as you said, there is a list of them. We give them about a paragraph treatment in each one, not in any detail.

Senator GILLIBRAND. Well, I would love for the record further development to the extent you have it.

Thank you.

Thank you, Mr. Chairman.

[The information referred to follows:]

Ambassador Edelman did not respond in time for printing. When received, answer will be retained in committee files.

Chairman MCCAIN. Senator Sessions?

Senator SESSIONS. Thank you, Mr. Chairman.

Thank both of you for your leadership and your wisdom that you are sharing with us.

We do have a problem with defense spending. It is causing me great concern as a member of the U.S. Senate Committee on Budget for a couple of years. I have been digging into those numbers, and I have felt all along that the one area of our budget that needs to be examined with most care for spending more money is the Defense Department. So, we have to justify that. The Defense Department has to tell us what they are going to spend the money on and how much it is.

But we don't have a lot of money. Matter of fact, we don't have enough money to run this government, and the deficits will continue to rise even though we have had a slowing on the annual deficits. They are going to start rising again, according to the Congressional Budget Office (CBO), and they project that by 2019, interest on the debt will exceed the entire defense budget. So this is a grim thing.

Ambassador Edelman, do you think—you have suggested that the Defense Department needs more money, do you think that increase above the BCA totals should be matched by the same increases of non-defense discretionary spending?

Ambassador EDELMAN. The panel did not take a position on that. So just as I represent the panel, I want to make sure it is clear that what I am about to say is my personal opinion and not representing, I suspect, either my colleague or other members of the panel.

I think the issue in defense is absolutely crucial. I think, overall, Federal spending needs to be under better control. I think the biggest problem, though, is frankly not the discretionary part of the budget. It is the nondiscretionary part.

The CBO long-range budget forecasts have made that clear for some time. That is the real driver of the long-term debt, three programs. Those have to be taken off.

Senator SESSIONS. Well, so is your answer yes or no?

Ambassador EDELMAN. My answer is that the defense budget needs to go up, and I don't think necessarily nondiscretionary—or rather, discretionary, non-defense spending needs to go up.

Senator SESSIONS. Well, look. The President is insisting that it does. His budget increases defense about $34 billion this year over the BCA level, and he increased his non-defense discretionary by the same.

Senator McCain, I think, was correct to suggest that the Gates plan would add, if it were enacted in 2012 and we were following it, it would be a $100 billion more this year than the BCA levels. Well, $100 billion more for defense over a decade is more than $1 trillion. Non-defense, if it is matched, that is another trillion dollars. The budget of the United States is $4 trillion.

So these are huge numbers, and all of us, you don't have the stress every day that we do about every other agency and department that comes to us and wants more money. I am just saying that is the difficult time we are in.

Ms. FLOURNOY. Senator, may I just add one thought on this?

Senator SESSIONS. Yes.

Ms. FLOURNOY. I think that sequestration needs to be lifted across the board so that Secretaries are able to manage to the priorities for the Government. But I don't think you can solve the Nation's budget problems on the back of discretionary spending. The big moving muscles are tax reform and entitlement reform. So, that is where I think we need to focus.

Senator SESSIONS. Well, under the BCA, beginning 2017, for the rest of, what, 7 years of the BCA, spending would increase at 2.5 percent a year. So it is not—these are the tough years. We are in the tough years right now. In fact, the Defense Department took a heavy, damaging demand to reduce spending so rapidly.

I thoroughly understand how hard they have had to work and the difficulties they are working with right now. But I don't know that we have to have these kind of increases in non-defense discretionary. It shows up, yes, the fastest-growing part of the budget is entitlements, and we all know that. But we can also make a difference with discretionary spending.

Ambassador Edelman, you have questioned, I think, the negotiations with Iran and the nuclear program they have. Dr. Henry Kissinger was pretty animated, really, when he expressed concern over our negotiating posture that basically allows Iran, as he understands it and public reports suggest, could be within months of having a nuclear weapon.

Our goal has gone from no nuclear program in Iran to allowing a nuclear program that would leave them within months of a nuclear weapon, causing, he says—Dr. Kissinger—other nations in the world and the region, like other nations, to plan to have nuclear weapons. How do you evaluate that?

Ambassador EDELMAN. Senator, I am a little concerned about the trajectory of these negotiations.

When you look at the full sweep of them going back to 2003, 2004, when it began as the European Union plus three before it became the sort of the P5+1, we started with what was essentially a multilateral negotiation with the objective of preventing Iran from developing a nuclear capability.

We now increasingly are in a bilateral negotiation between the United States and Iran that is aimed, as Secretary of State John F. Kerry has said, to limit the breakout or sneak-out time that Iran has to develop a nuclear weapon to 1 year. That seems to me to be an enormous retreat.

I don't know exactly what the state of the negotiation is. The press reports indicating that Iran might be allowed to keep thousands and thousands of centrifuges without taking them down is very, very concerning to me because I think because there is a time limit in the negotiation. That was agreed to in the joint plan of action. It will be time limited, whatever that date is, whether it is 20 years or 3 years or 10 years.

At some point, that time limit runs out. All the sanctions are gone. Iran is treated as a "normal nation" under the treaty on the Nonproliferation of Nuclear Weapons (NPT), despite its serial prevarication and violations of the NPT, and then they have an industrial-scale enrichment capability, which I think leaves them as a kind of threshold nuclear state. So I am very concerned about the way the negotiations have proceeded.

Chairman McCain. Senator Manchin?

Senator Manchin. Thank you, Mr. Chairman.

I want to thank both of our witnesses for their testimony before our committee today, and also your outstanding services, and the success you have had and the careers you have had with our Government.

In your opening statement, you both discussed the problems that sequestration is causing the Department. We have talked about that, and I am concerned the Department is not doing enough to streamline and reduce costs. That has been my concern.

In your panel's review of the 2014 QDR, you noted that additional changes are required to right-size the civilian Defense Department and Federal contracting workforces. The panel cited that Pentagon civilians continue to grow, even after, even after our Active-Duty Forces had been shrinking. Additionally, the panel noted that by 2012 the number of contractors working for the DOD had grown to approximately 670,000.

At a time when the Services have dramatically reduced the number of servicemembers in the military, I have a hard time with the growth of staff sizes, and I think you mentioned, Ms. Flournoy, the staff sizes. For example, just at the Army, headquarters staff grew by 60 percent to 3,639 in fiscal year 2013 from 2,272 just 10 years earlier. That doesn't even include the contractors.

Because of that, I was shocked, but perhaps not surprised, when the Government Accountability Office (GAO) recently reported that the DOD had yet to produce a realistic plan to meet Secretary Hagel's 2013 goal of reducing DOD headquarters budgets by 20 percent through fiscal year 2019. Can't even come to an agreement on that.

Additionally, the GAO found that the DOD headquarters they interviewed cannot determine how many people they actually needed. Couldn't even tell you what they needed and what positions they would have and what they would do.

Senators before this committee have heard time and again about the need to fully fund servicemembers in the field, and we are very concerned about that readiness of force. But when you have a bloat on the other side that is taking away from the readiness force, you are not utilizing the National Guard, you are basically not utilizing your reservists to the point that any sensible person would say, I have people ready, willing, and able to do the job, but yet I am hiring all these high-priced contractors.

There is no auditing going on. We don't really know where we stand. We can't get weapons to the front in time. We have concerns, and if either one of you want to address any of that to whatever specifics, I would appreciate it.

But it is a challenging thing to say, and I think all the Senators have touched on this, "We need more money. We need more money." We understand that. What are you doing with the money we give you?

Why are you throwing money away from the standpoint, or the appearance of it, spending it on needless stuff, when we want to make sure our readiness force is ready to do? They have the weapons, they can do the job for us.

Ms. FLOURNOY. Senator, I think this is a really important area of focus.

It is understandable at one level why the civilian workforce, the contract workforce grew over 15 years of war. But now I think it is time to sort of go back to first principles and try to right-size that force, examining exactly how contractors are being used, looking for efficiencies there, and really looking at the civilian organization. There is no overall plan, but there are some components that are taking some interesting approaches that may lead the way for others.

There are some that are looking at the concept of delayering, of reducing the number of layers and optimizing spans of control to take fat out of organizations. There are others who are looking at streamlining business processes, and so forth. So I think this is an area of focus.

One of the things I would highlight for you, although, is that currently the Secretary of Defense does not have the kind of authorities that his predecessors have used to manage drawdowns in this area. Secretary of Defense William J. Perry, for example, at the end of the Cold War, was given reduction-in-force authority to right-size the civilian workforce. He was given meaningful levels of voluntary separation incentive pays that can be used to incentivize early retirement.

The current Secretary does not have those authorities, and that is very much a constraint on——

Senator MANCHIN. So, legislative?

Ms. FLOURNOY. Yes, it is an opportunity for you to give the Secretary some additional tools to right-size that civilian workforce.

Senator MANCHIN. Let me ask you this. Does it not bother you that DOD can't even identify the types of jobs and the people they need for those jobs? Who reviews that? Who reviews that?

Ms. FLOURNOY. Yes. I think that is something that you need to ask of them and that we all need to ask of them.

Senator MANCHIN. Ambassador?

Ambassador EDELMAN. Senator Manchin, if I could just make a point to respond to I think the excellent question you have asked, but also the earlier question that Senator Sessions posed to us, which is we are coming here saying that DOD needs a lot of money, but everybody can cite horror stories about different procurements that have gone bad, different problems in DOD. You all, as stewards of the taxpayers' money, are right to be asking the department how to justify all this.

One of the things we do talk about in the report, and which my colleague has been very active, far more than I have, is on the entire reform agenda. There has just been a report by the Defense Business Board about trying to reap even more savings out of the department. This is a priority area, and I hope the chairman and the rest of you will have the Defense Business Board up and talk about that report and try and push the department and Secretary Carter, once he has gone to the floor and been confirmed, as well on all of these things. I know he has them very much on his mind from his previous service.

Senator MANCHIN. Thank you very much. My time is up.

Chairman McCAIN. Senator Ernst?

Senator ERNST. Thank you, Mr. Chair.

Thank you, Ms. Flournoy and Ambassador Edelman, for being here today. I appreciate it very much.

Ambassador, I appreciated when you said that we have been eating the seed corn. That comes home for me. But I truly do believe we have been degrading the very source of any future strength and readiness and prosperity that we have.

I do agree, Ms. Flournoy, you stated that we do need to end sequestration. I believe that. We do have to restore readiness and also aggressive reform within the DOD. We have to do that. I understand that.

But another component beyond looking internally, we have to look externally also. Anytime that the United States is engaging their military forces elsewhere, we do rely on other partners. I believe we do need to engage other partners in whatever region we are operating in to the fullest extent that we possibly can.

Over the last 12 years, military cooperation between the United States and Turkey has faltered. I can give specific examples at critical moments. Back in 2003, my own unit, the 1168th Transportation Company, the 4th Infantry Division, and many other units were denied access to Turkey as a projection platform into Iraq. So that is one example. We couldn't use their Turkish ports for Operation Iraqi Freedom.

Then just a few months ago, we saw Turkey deny our Kurdish allies from heading into Syria to break ISIL's siege of Kobane. I believe that led to many deaths for those that were trying to defend Kobane very early on when we were very uncertain whether Kobane was going to fall or not.

Then Turkey has also continuously denied our country the use of an air base, which would be close to use for search and rescue missions for those that might have issues if they fall behind enemy lines. Just recently, we saw a Wall Street Journal, too, that went into further detail how Turkey had denied us using their areas for Osprey, which could be used in those search and rescue missions and providing cover for men and women on the ground.

So time and time and time again, Turkey has denied use of their facilities, denied use of their grounds. They are a North Atlantic Treaty Organization (NATO) ally. A NATO ally, and they are very unapologetic when it comes to denying the resources we believe is necessary in their region.

So what I would like to hear from you is that as we are looking at constrained budgets here, lack of resources, and of course the reduced readiness, we really do need to engage our other partners, specifically Turkey. In your opinion, what impact has Turkey's actions or, in this case, lack of action, how has that affected other coalition partnership in that region, and what can we do to encourage Turkey to take on more ownership of the issues in the Middle East?

Ambassador EDELMAN. Senator Ernst, much as I would like to turn that question over to my colleague, I think as a former U.S. Ambassador to Turkey, I think I probably need to take it on.

First of all, all the things that you cited are painfully part of my past experience. There is just no question that Turkey under Prime Minister and now President Erdogan has become a very problematic and difficult ally. There are a lot of reasons for that.

I think Turkey is headed domestically on a very, very dangerous trajectory of increasing authoritarianism and a lot of degradation of democratic practice in Turkey, which I think contributes to some of this. I think it is going to require a lot of attention from senior U.S. leadership in the next few years to try and manage that relationship because I agree with you, we need partners when we operate overseas.

Now I will say in fairness to the Turks, a lot of their anger and unhappiness and some of the reason that they have denied us access is because their view of what is going on in Syria, with which they share a very long border, is that President Bashar al-Assad must go and that the United States is not doing enough to try and promote the departure of President Assad. It is their belief, and I think there is some merit in it, that you cannot just take on the problem in Syria by only taking on ISIL. Because as long as Assad is there, he is generating more recruitment and more support for ISIL with his assault on the Syrian people, use of barrel bombs, chlorine, et cetera.

I think that is a very large part of the Turkish frustration that has led them to deny us use of Incirlik, to not cooperate with us on combat search and rescue, and things like that. I am not saying that is an excuse, by the way. Because I think allies have disagreements, they don't then say we are not going to help you rescue your downed pilots. So I think that is not an excuse for Turkey's behavior in this instance, but just an explanation.

The broader point, though, on allies and partnerships that I think we have to wrestle with is we are at a junction because of where we are in our own budget and because the international order is fraying so badly, where we need our allies, our treaty allies in Asia and in Europe, but also our partners who are parts of special relationships, who may not be formally allies but clearly are partnered with us in various efforts in the Middle East, like Israel, like the Kingdom of Saudi Arabia, United Arab Emirates, et cetera.

In most cases, however, our allies are spending less and less and less on defense themselves, and so they have less and less capability for us to draw on. That is a sort of paradox.

I think one—I mean, it is a little bit beyond the work of our panel, but I do think one of the things we need to think about more is actually being much more forthright with our allies about where we want them to spend their money on defense and developing capabilities that will complement, supplement ours, replace areas where we may have less capabilities, so that there is a better division of labor between us and our allies. I think that is true in both Europe and in East Asia, as you see defense-spending declining in most of those countries. We need to do that so that we don't have them wasting money and not being able to be there when we need them.

Chairman McCAIN. Senator Donnelly?

Senator DONNELLY. Thank you, Mr. Chairman.

Thank you both for being here.

When you look at Syria and you look at ISIS, what would be your recommendation as to the next step for the coalition to take to move ISIS out of Syria?

We are making progress in Iraq. Do you wait in Syria until Iraq is done, or do you begin to take action right now to move them out, and does that action also include Assad?

Ambassador EDELMAN. I can answer that. This is again something that the panel, Senator Donnelly, did not look at.

Senator DONNELLY. I understand. But this is also about global strategy and national security.

Ambassador EDELMAN. Right. So, I am just—yes. No, I just want to make it clear that this is my personal opinion.

Senator DONNELLY. That is all I am asking.

Ambassador EDELMAN. It doesn't reflect the other members of the panel.

Senator DONNELLY. We have your presence here. I want to take advantage of it.

Ambassador EDELMAN. My own view is we should have been doing much more, much earlier. Again, the President has said long ago Assad must go. I agree with that. I don't think that there is any way this problem can be resolved as long as Assad is there.

Senator DONNELLY. What do you think we do now, moving forward?

Ambassador EDELMAN. I think we need—the problem in Syria is we are relying almost totally on air power. We have not very good intelligence because we have no presence on the ground. We have to find some kind of surrogate, as the Peshmerga have been to some degree in Iraq and, unfortunately, sometimes Shia militias in Iraq. We have to find a surrogate on the ground in Syria with whom we can work. That, I think, goes to the issue of arming of the moderate Syrian opposition and getting them into a position where they can actually do something.

We would have been much better off had we been doing this going back to 2011, rather than having to face this problem now. Bad news never gets better, in my experience.

Senator DONNELLY. Ms. Flournoy?

Ms. FLOURNOY. I would agree that we—I wish we would have begun arming of the moderate opposition when they were far stronger and in greater numbers a while back. But we are where we are, and I think building up a credible surrogate force is key.

I think the air campaign could be used in a more robust manner to put more pressure on ISIL and in some areas on the regime. I mean, the key is, eventually, you have to put pressure on the Assad regime if you expect them to come to the table.

If we were to do that and bring it to a culmination point right now, unfortunately, the main benefactor in Syria would be ISIL because they are the strongest force on the ground. So we have to focus on building up alternatives to ISIL and more moderate surrogates before we get to that point.

Senator DONNELLY. Let me ask you another question that is more about national security strategy, global strategy. That is

Vladimir Putin. What do you think his endgame is? If you can go one after the other, and where his plan ends here?

Ambassador EDELMAN. I don't think that President Putin is solely interested in the Donbass in Ukraine. I think he has a broader agenda. I think his agenda is first to destabilize Ukraine to the point that he can impose regime change in Kiev and dominate Ukraine and prevent it from associating itself with the European Union and moving in the direction of the West.

I think he fundamentally rejects the post-Cold War security order in Europe, and I think it has taken a while for a lot of our friends in Europe to recognize this. I think some of them are still in a bit of denial about it. They still seem to hope that there is some way to negotiate a limit with him on Ukraine.

But I think this is just the beginning. I think after Ukraine, he is going to—he is going to be pursuing this in Moldova, and I think we are likely to see efforts to create problems and drive wedges between the United States and its allies, and particularly its Baltic allies.

Senator DONNELLY. Would you agree that if NATO doesn't live up to its obligations in Latvia, that would be the end of NATO?

Ambassador EDELMAN. Absolutely.

Senator DONNELLY. Ms. Flournoy?

Ms. FLOURNOY. Yes, I don't disagree with anything that Ambassador Edelman said. But my sense is that Putin may not have a clear strategic endgame. He is a very tactical thinker, and he is sitting on top of a former great power that is unquestionably in decline demographically, economically, plagued by corruption, poor governance. But that doesn't make it any less dangerous, because I think he will lash out along the way, trying to reestablish his sphere of influence.

Senator DONNELLY. Do you think he takes a chance wherever he sees a weakness?

Ms. FLOURNOY. I do. I think that is why it is so important that we follow through on the reassurance initiatives for NATO, on our posture, bolstering our posture, underwriting Article 5 [of the Washington Treaty]. My own belief is that we should be doing more to help the Ukrainians defend themselves.

Senator DONNELLY. Thank you.

Thank you, Mr. Chairman.

Chairman MCCAIN. Senator Sullivan?

Senator SULLIVAN. Thank you, Mr. Chairman.

Again, I want to thank the panelists. Appreciate your great service to our country, and the joint statement, it is very helpful when we get those kind of joint statements.

We have been discussing a lot of the challenges, certainly, that we have as a country in terms of national security. We also have a lot of strengths. To me, the ultimate strength that we have is the men and women in uniform who continue to volunteer, raise their right hand, post-September 11 so they know what the risks are, to serve our country.

I have had the great honor, I get to spend a lot of time with our troops. I am sure that was a great part of both of your jobs. Just in the last 2 weekends, I was at the National Training Center a couple of weekends ago with thousands of young Alaskan soldiers training out there. This past weekend, I was with a smaller group of Air Naval, Gunfire Liaison Company marines, reservists, and this time with the troops for me raises a very interesting question I would like the two of you to maybe comment on.

What we hear from our civilian leaders a lot, President included, is that we consistently hear that we are a war-weary nation. There is a subtle element to that, I think, that it kind of is used as an excuse in some ways that we are not going to be taking any kind of action because we are weary.

But when you spend time with the troops, and they have sacrificed a lot in the last 12 years, we all know that. But one of the concerns that they raised, at least with me—and these are just anecdotal, but I am throwing them out there—is they want to deploy. They joined the military to serve their country. They don't want to be sitting around.

So I want you to help us think through this conventional wisdom that somehow we are a war-weary nation. We can't take on global commitments. When the truth is that less than 1 percent of Americans have actually been doing the fighting, and the ones that I am associated with certainly seem to be ready, not necessarily to fight, but certainly be ready to deploy.

How can we think through that? Because I think it is this issue that we are weary has become conventional wisdom in such a way that nobody seems to challenge it. When you talk to the people who are actually really at the pointy tip of the spear, God love them, they seem ready to go.

Ms. FLOURNOY. First of all, Senator, it is a great question, and I would agree that our men and women in uniform are one of the greatest strengths we have as a nation. They are remarkable.

I think that when the American people—when it is explained to the American people what the nature of a threat is, why we have to meet it, what it means for the Nation, what are the risks of not going after it, as the President did recently with regard to ISIL, I think the American people rally, and they may shed whatever weariness they have and support a cause when it is well articulated and explained, and the sacrifice or the risk seems commensurate with the importance of the interest.

So, I don't think we are generally war weary. I think, yes, we have spent—had a lot of blood and treasure that we have spent over the last 15 years. But when I think when—and that is something that weighs heavily on everyone, as it should.

But I think, again, when the interests are clear, the objectives are clear, the mission is clear, and it is well explained and people are mobilized, I think they are very willing to follow that strong instinct that you described in the troops of we have a mission, and we need to get it done.

Senator SULLIVAN. Yes.

Ms. FLOURNOY. So I think that is the challenge for everyone who is in a leadership—public leadership position to be making that case when it is necessary.

Senator SULLIVAN. Ambassador?

Ambassador EDELMAN. General George C. Marshall, I think, once said that he thought it was difficult, if not impossible, for the United States to fight a war for more than 4 years.

I think what that reflects is that Americans tend to want to see—they tend to want to see a decisive outcome to a conflict. I think inconclusive wars and long, difficult fights sometimes can be a bit exhausting to the public, and particularly if, as my colleague suggested, they are not being explained properly to the American public.

I agree with everything you said, Senator Sullivan, about being credible, the comparative advantage with have with our people. It was always incredibly inspiring to go to either Iraq or Afghanistan and see our young folks out there. They are truly incredible and doing incredible things.

I would frequently, when I talked to folks, particularly enlisted, and say do you think people out here—do you think people back home know what you are doing out here? The answer I used to get was, no, they think all we do is step on improvised explosive devices out here. They have no clue what we are doing.

So I do think it is important to explain exactly what the stakes are, as my colleague just said. I would also note one other thing. Americans are war weary until they are not.

If you look at the poll data about how the public felt after the videotapes of the beheadings this summer came out, it was a very different set of numbers than what you had seen previously because Americans feel these things very deeply and see them as a sign of disrespect to the Nation, which they don't appreciate.

Senator SULLIVAN. Thank you.

Thank you, Mr. Chairman.

Chairman MCCAIN. Senator King?

Senator KING. Thank you, Mr. Chairman.

Just to put into perspective the numbers that we were talking about at the beginning and looking back on the history. If we had the Gates budget of 2012, the defense budget this year would be somewhere around $612 billion, 3.4 percent of gross domestic product (GDP). Instead, under the sequester level, we are at $492 billion, 2.8 percent of GDP, which is just about the lowest level of GDP since World War II.

It is also—it is the lowest level of Federal spending, lowest percentage of Federal spending for defense since World War II. Four percent, which is a kind of post-World War II average, would be $700 billion, almost $100 billion more.

So we are definitely at a very low point in terms of funding of defense at a time of escalating challenge on multiple fronts. So I just—I think putting it in percentage of GDP is a sort of good way to look at it, because it really puts it in historical perspective.

A question for both of you. Ambassador, you have mentioned about arming the Ukrainians, and that seems to be a developing consensus here in Washington that that is something we ought to do. I understand that, and I understand the precedent of the Sudetenland, and if there had been force in 1939, we might have avoided the catastrophe of World War II. On the other hand, I also understand the precedent of the guns of August and stumbling into a catastrophic world war.

We are playing chess with a Russian here. Now if you play chess with a Russian, you better think two and three moves ahead. My concern is: (A) Russia has a historic paranoia about encroachment from the west; and (B) Putin probably wouldn't mind a manageable little war in Ukraine right now to take the people's minds off of the domestic problems.

Margaret Thatcher's approval rating the day before the Falklands War was 23 percent. Two weeks later, it was 70 percent. I suspect Putin may not know those numbers, but he knows the phenomenon.

Persuade me that the escalation by arming the Ukrainians would not lead to a matching escalation and, in fact, an increase. We don't live in a static world. We can't assume that we arm the Ukrainians. Putin says, "Oh, this is tough. I am going home." He is not responsive to bodies in bags or tightening sanctions.

Give me your thoughts.

Ambassador EDELMAN. Well, a couple of things. I know my colleague will want to speak to this because she, with some other colleagues, has just been a signatory to a very good paper on this subject that Brookings Institution, Atlantic Council, and the Chicago Council on World Affairs, I guess, or Foreign Affairs, has put out.

I think your question is a good one, Senator King, and it has to be answered, I would say, at multiple levels.

First, it is true that in some sense President Putin has what we used to call in the Cold War escalation dominance in Ukraine. The stakes are higher for him. The region is closer. He has more force.

Senator KING. He has more chips.

Ambassador EDELMAN. He has more chips, exactly.

Having said that, he is also signatory, his country is signatory, to a number of agreements that make it clear that countries have a right to belong to whatever alliance or multilateral organizations like the European Union that they would like to associate with. So——

Senator KING. Do you seriously believe Putin cares about agreements?

Ambassador EDELMAN. No. But we should. We should care about it. The point is that he doesn't have a legitimate way to protest that we are helping a legitimate government defend itself against his aggression. I think we have to think about it in terms of the moral obligation to do that. When people want to defend themselves, we have an obligation, I think, to try to help them if we can.

I think, second, we need to raise the cost for him of what he is doing. He, I think, is perhaps a little bit more sensitive to some of these things than you were suggesting. The body bags coming home. The protesting Russian mothers. The capital flight. The amount of money that has been expended defending the ruble. These are real costs, and they are costs that are hitting his base of support, which is the oligarchs. They are suffering from this, and so he has to respond to that in some way.

But I think it is also important to remember that while there are potentially costs to action, there are very serious costs to inaction here.

Senator KING. Sure. There are risks either way.

Ambassador EDELMAN. The cost to inaction could be, I would suggest, a catastrophic miscalculation. We need to make him understand that if we are willing to provide this kind of assistance to a country with whom we have no treaty legal obligation, that he ought to think twice then about doing something with a NATO member state like Latvia, as Mr. Donnelly asked me about earlier, with whom we do have a legal treaty obligation.

It is the importance of underscoring our commitment to defend our NATO allies in Europe that really is at stake here, I think. If we don't do this, the risk that he will miscalculate in a place like Latvia or Estonia I think will go up dramatically. I think that is something in terms of regret that we will feel very seriously later on.

Senator KING. My father used to say, there lies the body of Jonathan Gray, who died defending his right of way. But in any case.

Ms. FLOURNOY. I would just add that I think one of the things that we have learned since the collapse of the ceasefire is that Putin is going to continue to escalate because he wants to keep destabilizing Ukraine and eventually cause the regime to change. So he is on an escalatory path anyway.

The question is whether we can provide Ukraine, Ukrainians with the weapons they need to impose a level of cost on the separatists and their Russian backers that might make him think twice. Particularly counter-battery radars that could locate where the artillery and rocket fire is coming from. That is what is responsible for 70 percent of the casualties in Ukraine. Anti-tank systems that could stop armored or heavy-armored vehicles from taking further territory.

So I think he has demonstrated he is on an escalatory path. The question is whether there is anything that we can do to help Ukraine impose costs to make him stop and actually come to the negotiation seriously.

I think it is worth seeing what happens on Wednesday in Minsk and seeing if by some miracle an agreement is forged. But barring that, I think it is very important that we help the Ukrainians defend themselves and impose greater costs on the separatists and the Russians for their aggression.

Senator KING. Thank you. Very helpful.

Chairman MCCAIN. Senator Ayotte?

Senator AYOTTE. I want to thank both of you for being here.

Secretary Flournoy, I wanted to ask you about Afghanistan. I know that last June you were quoted in the New York Times about the administration's timeline for withdrawal from Afghanistan. And one of the things you said was, ''If it was a timeline with a strong statement that said, hey, this is our plan, but no plan survives contact with reality, and of course, we are going to adjust based on conditions on the ground, then no problem.'' In reference to their withdrawal plan.

''Are the Afghans on the path we had planned for? Are they not? Is the insurgency as we expected or is it worse? All those things have to be factored in. What I am hearing out of the White House is that it is hell or high water. This is what we are going to do.''

I'm hoping that you have a different sense of this now, and I wanted to get your thoughts on Afghanistan because many of us, I think, who have had the opportunity to visit Afghanistan, and then this weekend, we had obviously the opportunity to sit down with President Ghani and hear his perspective, to really understand their plan right now as it stands. President Ghani seemed very concerned that we not reduce our forces in 2015, in particular. Then many of us are very concerned that by the end of 2016 under the current plan, it will really be 1,000 people based in Kabul.

So I wanted to get your perspective on Afghanistan and what you think we should be doing.

Ms. FLOURNOY. So that is a great question. Thank you, Senator, for asking.

I think at this point we need to change the frame of discussion on Afghanistan. Rather than debating the fine points of the final phases of the drawdown and the end of the U.S. combat role and so forth, we need to stop and say, okay, we need to look forward.

We have an Afghan Government that is trying—has a good chance of pulling it together and going forward as a democratically-elected coalition government. We have an Afghan National Security Force (ANSF) that is continuing to develop its capabilities that is in the fight, that is taking risk, that is trying to hold their ground.

But we also see continued challenge from an insurgency that remains able to contest a lot of areas. We see continued activity from al Qaeda moving across, back and forth across the border.

So now is the time to stop debating whether we can change the drawdown timeline, and we need to stop and say, okay, looking forward, what kind of posture does the United States need, both intelligence and military, in the Armed Forces Pacific region to protect ourselves against future terrorist threats and prevent Afghanistan or the border region from becoming a serious safe haven once again for al-Qaeda and associated groups?

With that fresh sheet of paper, look at what is the intelligence posture we need, what is the military posture we need to support that and to continue to help the Afghan national forces to develop. I think that shift in the conversation is very, very important.

My sense is that it is starting to happen inside, certainly inside the Intelligence Community. But hopefully, that is a conversation we need to have over the next year.

Senator AYOTTE. Could you give, I think, thinking about our constituents, the importance of really looking forward there and frankly, in terms of our own interests, the importance of Afghanistan and the intelligence that we might need from Afghanistan for protecting our own interests?

Ms. FLOURNOY. This is an area where we need to continue to be able to have a sense of what the remnants of al Qaeda that remain there, their Taliban supporters, the Haqqani network. We need to still have eyes and ears. It is not something you can do from Kabul alone or from Bagram alone.

That intelligence posture will require some supporting military posture. It will be far less than what we have had in previous years. It is a small continued investment, relatively speaking, to try to support the Afghan Government in continuing on the path of progress and continuing to hold their country and not allow the insurgency to regain any kind of foothold in terms of actually governing or leading the country.

Senator AYOTTE. Thank you.

I also wanted to follow up briefly with the size of the naval fleet, including the attack submarines. As I understand it, with sequester we are on a path really to reduce our fleet size to 260 ships or less overall. Having worked on the QDR, the Navy's current fleet size is around 285. As I look at the attack submarine fleet size, this is something that we have even greater need for now, especially as we want to have a presence in the Asia-Pacific region.

So I wanted to get your assessment of, as we go forward, where we are—it looks like a dramatic decline if we continue on sequester—the importance of the attack submarine fleet, and this investment and why it is important for us.

Ms. FLOURNOY. I think, overall, the fleet is on a path to becoming too small for what we will need in the future. I agree with you that undersea warfare is an area of American advantage that we want to do everything in our power to keep.

I think that will require continued investment in the attack submarine fleet, but it is also going to require investment in new technologies, such as unmanned undersea vehicles and how we network manned submarines and unmanned systems to leverage that capability to have much greater impact. So I think this is an area very ripe for some new thinking and development of—both leveraging of new technologies and developing of new operational concepts.

But your core premise about the importance of the attack submarine fleet, I think it is a very important advantage area that we want to maintain.

Senator AYOTTE. Thank you.

Ambassador EDELMAN. Senator, if I could just add, we did not have the kind of staffing that would have enabled us to do a real fine-grain analysis of this. But we did conclude, as you have suggested in your question, as my colleague just suggested in her answer, that we are on a path towards a fleet that is much too small and that we ought to—we tried to bracket the problem for you and your colleagues by saying, somewhere between the number that Secretary Gates requested in the fiscal year 2012 budget, which I think was 320 something, and the number Secretary Perry identified in the bottom-up review, which was in the 340s, was the place where we ought to be looking to try and get.

Senator AYOTTE. Thank you.

Chairman MCCAIN. Senator Shaheen?

Senator SHAHEEN. Thank you, Mr. Chairman, and again thank you for holding this series of rather strategic looks at what our defense capabilities should be going forward.

I want to thank both of our panelists for being here and for your long service to this country.

Follow up—first, I should apologize for missing your statements and the earlier questions. I was at a briefing on Iran and those negotiations. But I wanted to follow up on Senator Ayotte's question because I am not sure if she asked very directly if, in your assessment, should we be drawing down troops, the remaining troops, in Afghanistan as rapidly as we are this year?

Or do you think that sends the wrong message to both the Afghans, who are trying to make a new start with a new president and address their internal issues, as well as the Taliban and the other enemies who are fighting them in Afghanistan?

Ms. FLOURNOY. My sense is that the delay in the government formation process that we have seen post-elections in Afghanistan should put some more time on the clock in terms of the drawdown, and we need to re-examine that.

But most fundamentally, what I was trying to say before is that we need to re-examine the pace and scope of the drawdown in light what we are going to need in the future. I don't believe a zero posture in Afghanistan is going to serve our interests in the long term, given the continued terrorism threats that we face, given the continued importance of our support to the development of the ANSF.

So figuring out, instead of from looking back and drawing down, looking forward and saying what are we going to need in the next 5 to 10 years? It will be more modest than what it has been, certainly, but it won't be zero. So, figuring out what that look like and having that inform the pace and scope of the final stages of the drawdown, I think, is very important.

Senator SHAHEEN. Ambassador Edelman, did you agree?

Ambassador EDELMAN. Senator Shaheen, you have asked a very good question, and I am very concerned that we are going to go down too low. I mean, I think it is a source of great regret, I think, to most of us that we left Iraq without any residual presence. The consequences, I think, are staring us in the face, with the rise of ISIL, collapse of the Iraqi security forces. I worry that we may be putting ourselves on the same path in Afghanistan, and I hope we won't do that.

Senator SHAHEEN. Well, thank you both.

With respect to Europe and what is happening in Ukraine, how important is the effort to beef up NATO, to encourage the European countries to actually follow through on their commitment to provide 2 percent of GDP for support for NATO?

To what extent do you think actually doing that, actually taking some of these steps with NATO to put more visible operations on the borders of Eastern Europe, will be helpful in deterring Russia from future aggression?

Ms. FLOURNOY. I think it is absolutely critical. There is a clear plan to bolster our posture, exercise activity, our cooperation, our pre-positioning, with our NATO allies, particularly the front-line states, Baltics, Poland, and so forth. I think doing that consistently, reliably, visibly is extremely important to bolstering deterrence and to reassuring our allies.

I also think that getting more of our allies to meet the 2 percent of GDP defense spending target is essential, as is engaging them as partners in developing capabilities for the future. We talk about an offset strategy and innovation agenda. We need to have that on a transatlantic basis as well, with some great opportunities for pooling resources, sharing, having a clearer division of labor, and so forth.

Senator SHAHEEN. I know that you both were in Munich this past weekend. To what extent did you hear NATO members, countries who were there, talking about their appreciation that this is important for them as well, if at all?

Ambassador EDELMAN. Well, Senator Shaheen, there was actually, I thought, not very much of that. I heard a lot of discussion about how there is no military solution to the problem in Ukraine. That is, I think, demonstrably false. If we do nothing, there will be military solution in Ukraine, and it is going to be the one that is imposed by Vladimir Putin.

I think the importance of all the things, and I agree with everything that my colleague said about the importance of the NATO reassurance effort and all of that, in terms of deterrence. I think we also need to remember it is an important part of diplomacy.

I always carry around with me a quotation from George Kennan, who says, you have no idea—this was a lecture he gave to the National War College in 1946—how much it contributes to the general politeness and pleasantness of diplomacy when you have a little quiet armed force in the background. I think that we tend to lose track of that.

I mean, what is now going on, and I hope maybe there will be some success to it on Wednesday, but we should be clear about what is happening. The Europeans are discussing this and calling it ''Minsk Plus.'' But it is really ''Ukraine Minus'' because what it does is it reaffirms the principles of the Minsk Agreement in September but makes adjustment for the reality of the continued aggression by the Donbass separatists.

We should have no illusions about what is happening here, and it is the reason why I think I—I am not going to speak for my colleague, but why I believe we do need to, on the Ukrainian Government, to raise the cost to President Putin.

I will say, and Senator King has raised this and raised rightly the question of how do we respond to further escalation by President Putin? One thing I think is absolutely important to bear in mind, which is if we do this, we have to do this seriously.

We cannot arm the Ukrainian Government the way we have been arming the Syrian moderate opposition for the last 3 years. Because if we do that, we will end up with all the effective provocation of President Putin, with none of the benefit of increased deterrence or military capability for Ukraine.

Senator SHAHEEN. Thank you both.

Chairman MCCAIN. Senator Hirono?

Senator HIRONO. Thank you, Mr. Chairman.

I would like to be noted as voting in person for Dr. Carter.

Chairman MCCAIN. Without objection.

Senator HIRONO. Thank you.

Thank you both for your testimony and your service.

Secretary Flournoy, I do appreciate your noting that there is a shift in the conversation that is beginning regarding what we need to do in Afghanistan, and certainly in the Intelligence Community that this shift is happening. I think that moves us forward, as opposed to talking about what we should have done, et cetera.

I also would like to thank both of you for stressing the important of maintaining our sea power and your concerns about our decreasing size of our fleet. Dr. Carter was asked at his confirmation, and I would like to paraphrase the question he was asked. He was asked how do we respond to the threats in the Middle East and Africa, Ukraine, and still be committed to the rebalance to the Asia-Pacific?

I would like to ask both of you the same question, but first, why you believe that the rebalance is important to our national security.

Ms. FLOURNOY. Well, let me start it since I can be blamed for part of that—part of that initiative.

When you look long term at what region of the world will have the greatest impact on U.S. economic prosperity and, I think, our security, Asia-Pacific is undeniably sort of the most important. So, it speaks to even though we obviously have to deal with crises in the Middle East, we have to deal with Russian aggression in Europe, over the arc of the long term we want to be ensuring that we are adequately investing in Asia, in the foundations of continued economic growth, in the maintenance of the rules-based international order that has been underwriting stability there, in our alliances, in our partnerships.

So I think it is very important that the rebalance continue not only militarily shifting more of our assets there and becoming—investing more with our partnerships and alliances there, but also in economic terms. I think this is why the Trans-Pacific Partnership is such an important initiative, to signal U.S. commitment to the region, U.S. staying power, that the United States will remain a critical economic partner as well as a security partner going forward.

Senator HIRONO. Mr. Ambassador?

Ambassador EDELMAN. The region obviously is growing in wealth and importance in the world, and obviously America's future is very much tied up. We have always been an Atlantic and a Pacific nation, but the impact of the Pacific is much greater now and will be in the future for some time to come.

I think it is for that reason that all the members of the panel agreed that the general direction that the President announced in the Defense Strategic Guidance in January 2012 was the right direction. I think what we expressed in the report is some concern about whether at current budget levels this will be sustainable, and that is why we talked about the importance of growing both naval and air capability because this is a theater where largely we are going to be operating in and because of the tyranny of distance and geography over water and air.

So I think the need is clear. I think it is important that we move ahead on the rebalance. I am concerned that what we have done already is fairly limited. On the military side, it is—and I am not saying that we shouldn't do it, but it is basically 2,500 marines rotationally deployed to Darwin, 4 littoral combat ships home ported in Singapore, and some rebalancing of a shrinking fleet.

I think we need to do more, and it is one of the reasons I think we believe we have to lift the BCA caps and sequestration.

Senator HIRONO. Thank you.

Mr. Ambassador, you noted in a response to one of the questions earlier asked that other nations are decreasing the amount of resources they are putting into the military.

Would you say that that is where Japan is also?

Ambassador EDELMAN. Under Prime Minister Shinzo Abe, Japan has obviously done a bit to increase its defense capabilities. I don't think they have done enough, and we need to make sure that the money they spend—I mean, Japan spends about 1 percent of its GDP on defense, which is, given the size of the Japanese economy, a considerable amount of money.

I think where we need to help our allies in Japan is working with them, as I said earlier in response to one of the questions, to focus on the capabilities we think they can provide that will really be additive and help complement what we are doing. That is what I think we ought to be doing with Japan.

I think Prime Minister Abe has done a lot to change the direction in Japan in a more positive direction.

Senator HIRONO. Mr. Chairman, may I just ask the Secretary to respond to that, too?

Ms. FLOURNOY. I would agree that I think Japan is moving in the right direction. I think Prime Minister Abe is seeking to have an internal discussion that will allow the Japanese military to play a more fulsome role as a full partner in our alliance.

I think that the depth of the alliance relationship is really unprecedented now, and we are deeply engaged in looking at the region, developing common understandings of the environment, the threats we see, the capabilities that are needed, how we will invest together, and so forth. So I actually think the alliance is on a very strong footing and moving in the right direction.

But the question really is the internal debate within Japan about the proper role of the military and what the Japanese people are comfortable with moving forward.

Senator HIRONO. Thank you.

Thank you, Mr. Chairman.

Chairman MCCAIN. Senator Kaine?

Senator KAINE. Thank you, Mr. Chairman, and thank you to the witnesses.

I also want to be noticed. I was a proxy 'yes' for Ash Carter, but I am a proud 'yes' now that I am here from my Foreign Relations meeting.

Thank you for your testimony, especially your strong testimony with respect to the foolishness of the sequester in today's global environment.

Big picture strategic question, since you are both good strategic thinkers. I know questions have been asked earlier about Afghanistan. We are grappling with—and we will have hearing on Afghanistan later in the week—should our activities be based on a calendar or based on conditions on the ground? Those questions have been asked already.

But from a strategic standpoint, talk about what failure in Afghanistan would mean. If we were to pull out precipitously, for example, and then the gains that we have achieved are lost, what would that mean to U.S. credibility? What would it mean to the people of Afghanistan? What would it mean in the region from a security standpoint?

Ms. FLOURNOY. Well I can start. I think, if history is any guide, it could be very dangerous for the Afghan Government and Afghan society.

Recall that when the Soviets ended their aid to the Afghan Government, the government collapsed. I think if the United States were to have and the international community were to have no follow-on mission in NATO, that international assistance would quickly dry up, and you could see a sort of accelerated decline of the Afghan Government's hold over territory and the country. So I think it would be very, very dangerous.

On the opportunity side, I think with continued modest, but consistent international support, I think the Afghan Government has an opportunity to hold the key urban centers, the ring road, the strategic territory inside Afghanistan, and keep governing without having the government and the overall control of the country being threatened by a continued insurgency.

Given that this region remains a home to various terrorist elements that still harbor very dire intentions, dangerous intentions against the United States, it is some place we have to keep an eye on and keep investing in to make sure those threats are kept at bay.

So I think the stakes are very high. I also think it would be very damaging for U.S. credibility to have put so much into getting Afghanistan to the point where it is today and then to pull the carpet out from underneath their feet. I think it would also be very damaging in terms of civil-military relations, given the degree of sacrifice that our men and women have been asked to make, to create the possibility for Afghanistan to succeed and then to walk away from that before we complete the job I think would be very, very damaging.

Senator KAINE. Ambassador Edelman, quickly, I have one more question, but would there be something you would want to add to that?

Ambassador EDELMAN. I agree. The reputational risk. The homeland risk because it will become ungoverned space again. I would add one other thing. It will reduce our strategic leverage on Pakistan, and we should not lose sight of the large number of nuclear weapons that Pakistan presides over.

Senator KAINE. One other question. The big picture strategy sense. I was a mayor worrying about my police force. I was a governor worrying about economic development. But you guys have been doing national security for your whole career, so I want to hear your thoughts on this.

We often hear questions in these hearings about where is the strategy? And I am kind of sympathetic to those questions. As I look kind of quickly at what we have been up to, we had a national security strategy, like it or not. The Truman Doctrine from 1946 until the Soviet Union collapsed. I think we then went into kind of an ad hoc-ism period. That may not be a bad thing, but we kind of dealt with challenges as they arose and often not in consistent ways.

September 11 began. Our policy was the war on terror. That is not a big enough national security policy for a nation as great as the United States, as magnanimous as the United States. And so, I think we are probably now recognizing the ongoing battle with terror, still looking for a broader definition of what is a big picture national strategy.

Are we back to a sort of ad hoc-ism? Or as folks who have done this for a lifetime professionally, what would you suggest to us the big picture national security strategy should be?

Ms. FLOURNOY. To me? This is the $64,000 question. I think that it is something, we have to rise above the crisis of the day and get back to having a strategic framework, a sense of American purpose in the world that can garner bipartisan support.

I personally believe that one of the key elements of it is to defend the international rules-based order that we put into place, we architected after World War II, that has been the basis for stability in so many regions, and it has been the basis for our economic growth and our security.

We have a lot riding on that, and it is being challenged in Asia with the rise of China that is questioning that order and challenging and trying to unilaterally change the status quo. It is being challenged in the Middle East as the boundaries of nation-states start to fray, and you have Sunni-Shia conflict, the rise of extremist terrorist elements. Now it is being challenged in the heart of Europe with Russian aggression across an international border.

So I think sustaining that rules-based international order is something that has to be at the heart of any strategic framework we develop.

Senator KAINE. Mr. Chair, could I ask Ambassador Edelman just to answer that question as well?

Ambassador EDELMAN. Well, I agree with everything that my colleague said, Senator Kaine. So that makes it a little bit easier.

A few years ago, there was an article in the journal International Security that had the provocative title of ``Strategy is an Illusion.'' I teach a course in American grand strategy at Johns Hopkins University, School of Advanced International Studies, and my students at the end of it, some of them say, ``well, yes, it was easy to have a strategy when you had a bipolar world and one adversary. Now it is just so complicated. It is too hard.''

As Secretary Flournoy and I said in our opening statement that we are dealing with a volatile and complex security environment, and therefore, maybe you might just say, well, it is too hard to do.

My view is that as hard as it may be, marrying objectives to ways and means is just the essence of good governance, and if you don't try to do it, it just becomes an excuse for going, taking any road that will lead you where you think you might want to go, but you won't have a road map. So I think it is a necessity. I think we have to do it.

I think there is a lot of merit in what Secretary Kissinger has suggested, that we need to—we are faced by primarily regional challengers now, not a global peer competitor. We need to develop regional strategies, but strategies that are interconnected with an overarching global vision, and I think that is the beginning of wisdom on that subject.

Senator KAINE. Thank you.

Thank you, Mr. Chairman.

Chairman MCCAIN. I do recall a thing called the Reagan Doctrine, which in the words of Margaret Thatcher, won the Cold War without firing a shot. But maybe there are some of us who have different views of history.

Senator Sullivan, did you have an additional question?

Senator SULLIVAN. Thank you, Mr. Chairman.

I just had one quick follow-up question, and it relates to some of the broader issues that we are struggling with here. I would like your views on just some of the—your thoughts on what is going to be looks like an upcoming debate in Congress on the authorization for use of military force (AUMF).

Secretary Flournoy, you mentioned a fresh start looking forward. How would you advise Members of Congress to look at that, whether it is years, troops, geographic scope? There is a lot that can go into something like that. It is going to be important, and I would just appreciate your views on that.

Thank you, Mr. Chairman.

Ms. FLOURNOY. First of all, I would say I think it is important to have the discussion. The debate about the AUMF will be a good surrogate for what should our strategy be with regard to counterterrorism and with regard to the Middle East.

I think that as you have that discussion, it is very important to remember something that was said earlier, which is we are very bad at predicting exactly how conflicts are going to unfold, how enemies are going to act, how things are going to morph and change. So, being overly restrictive, saying categorically no boots on the ground, or don't do this. Being overly restrictive, I think, could become a problem over time.

That said, I think it is very, very important to recognize that the AUMF that we have from 2001, a lot of realities have moved beyond that, and we do need to update it and recognize that there are groups who have distanced themselves from al Qaeda but, nevertheless, now pose a similar threat to us. We need to have an authorization to deal with them.

But again, I would just caution against being overly predictive or specific in restrictions because we don't exactly know how the threat will evolve, how our response will need to evolve.

Ambassador EDELMAN. Senator Sullivan, I agree with that. I agree with everything that Michéle just said.

I would just add that the other element here is I know that there is lots of interest in some kind of timeline. We frequently talk about this. I think that to do that is to set up potentially a very divisive and a difficult debate later on down the road.

Things don't always work out in war. There are mistakes, and you have problems. You have to let the people who are fighting the war fight the war. I think you also don't want to signal lack of resolve to the other side and tell them how long they have to wait you out.

Senator SULLIVAN. Thank you, Mr. Chairman.

Chairman MCCAIN. Well, I thank you, the witnesses, and we have covered a wide range of issues today.

Senator SHAHEEN. Mr. Chairman, can I ask another question before we close?

Chairman MCCAIN. The Senator from New Hampshire.

Senator SHAHEEN. Thank you.

I wanted to follow up on Senator Kaine's question about strategy because there have been a number of high-profile articles in the last few months about the lessons learned in Afghanistan and Iraq, and there has been the DOD-commissioned report from the RAND Corporation about those lessons learned that have suggested that we ought to also take a look at our decisionmaking structures and think about how we can better make some of those decisions.

I wonder if I could get each of you to comment on whether you think that is an accurate analysis of some of the challenges that we face and what we should do better as we are thinking about how to make these decisions in the future.

Ms. FLOURNOY. I think it is really important to try to pause and catalogue what lessons we should be learning. There is kind of a desire to get all of this in the rearview mirror and just move on. But it is very, very important to understand what we should take away from this and capture some of the best practices that were developed on the ground. So I think it is an important exercise.

I do think that the decisionmaking element, particularly at the interagency level, is something that bears study. It is something that actually the Center for New American Security is looking at going forward because I think you can look at different models of National Security Councils, different ways in which they have operated, different results over time and history, and you can draw some conclusions about what works better and what doesn't.

Similarly, I think in the field, some of the innovations for fusing intelligence and operations and having all of the interagency players in one operations center, sharing authorities, information, and conducting truly joint whole-of-government operations, that is something we don't want to lose, the next time we may have to face an operational challenge.

So I think it is a really important line of inquiry.

Ambassador EDELMAN. Senator Shaheen, I have to confess to a certain degree of skepticism about reforming the interagency process. It is a little bit like the weather. People are always talking about it, and then it doesn't ever change.

The National Security Act of 1947 is an incredibly flexible—has created an incredibly flexible system. The reality is that it is flexible enough that each President that we have had has developed a system that suits their management style best and for better or for worse.

Our system is so presidential-centric in terms of national security decisionmaking that I think unless you really want to tinker with the Constitution, I am not sure that anything else that you do is going to be more than moving kind of boxes around on a wiring diagram. So I think it is certainly worth looking at lessons learned, and there are always better or worse ways to do it.

But I am struck by the fact that the relationship between process and outcome is not always clear and direct. If you read through, for instance, the transcripts of the Executive Committee of the National Security Council during the Cuban missile crisis and were graded on process, you would give it an F, because there are no agendas. They are not talking from common papers. They are not doing anything that they teach you to do at the Kennedy School of Government, for instance.

But President Kennedy came roughly to the right decision, obviously, somehow. I think that is just testimony to what I was saying. This is a system that really ultimately revolves around the President, and he or she, I think, should not necessarily be constrained by efforts to tinker with the machinery.

Senator SHAHEEN. Thank you both.

Thank you, Mr. Chairman.

Chairman MCCAIN. Your testimony has been very helpful. We began our conversations about your work on a commission, and now we have branched out and covered a lot of very important areas that I think that needs to be an important part of the discussion and dialogue that we have on both sides of the aisle and both ends of Pennsylvania Avenue.

So you have contributed a great deal to our knowledge and our thought process, and I thank you for it.

Jack?

Senator REED. I simply want to express the same feeling of appreciation for your efforts not just today, but for many, many years. Thank you very much.

Chairman MCCAIN. Thank you.

The hearing is adjourned.

[Whereupon, at 11:31 a.m., the committee adjourned.]